The Gallbladder Diet
(US Edition)

MEAT, FISH & SEAFOOD

EASY, LOW-FAT RECIPES FOR A HEALTHY LIFE AFTER GALLBLADDER REMOVAL SURGERY

by Iris Pilzer

CONTENTS

Lean Poultry

Caesar's salad with chicken	8
Chicken ragout Ohio	12
Chicken ragout with tomatoes	12
Chicken skewers in peanut sauce	10
Chicken with stewed vegetables	10
Farfalle with chicken and tomatoes	14
Glass noodle salad with chicken breast	16
Kentucky salad	16
Salad with chicken breast	8
Turkey wraps	14

Crispy Pork

Bean & ham salad	18
Eggplant pan	20
Fried chorizo with herbs	24
Ground meat with beans	20
Lasagna	22
Mini pork skewers	18
Pasta with ham and peas	24

Finest Beef

Avocado & steak pan	28
Zucchini noodles with ground beef	34
Glass noodles with steak	34
Ground meat with soybean sprouts	26
Meat & tomato pot with spinach	30
Meat balls with strawberry salsa	30
Onions with ground beef	26
Steak sandwich	28
Steak wraps with salsa and guacamole	32

Spicy Seafood

Garlic shrimps	38
Pasta casserole with seafood	36
Pasta salad with seafood	36
Puff pastry with shrimp filling	40
Salad with calamari	38
Shrimp & melon wraps	42
Shrimp & vegetable salad	40
Vegetable noodles with shrimps	42

Rich Fish

Adriatic fish stew	50
Asian salmon with sprout salad	46
Chinese fish sticks	50
Salad with salmon cubes	46
Smoked salmon toast avocado	48
Smoked salmon toast egg	48
Smoked salmon wraps	44
Warm tomato salad with salmon	44

NOVEMBER 2017, MY LIFE WAS OVER.

I had an awful pain in my stomach area. The only thing I wanted to do was to cower in my bed and die. My doctor's diagnosis: gall- stones. Lots of them. Which had shut down my life for the past 6 month without me knowing what was wrong. I had surgery late November. A laparoscopic cholecystectomy. In layperson's terms: my gallbladder was removed. And two days later I was discharged from hospital with the sound advice that I should eat low-fat food from now on.

Of course, this suggestion was most helpful (please note my sarcasm). Until then, fat was an important part of my diet. The human body needs fat. And women in particular need a certain amount of fat every day to stay healthy. And now the doctors and nurses were telling me that, suddenly, I should stop eating fat?

O.K., I found out pretty quickly that too much fat isn't good for me. My liver still continues to produce bile, but I don't have a gallbladder anymore to store bile for the times when I eat a lot of fat. And, as it turned out, this had a rather unpleasant effect on my digestion.

On the plus side: I really like to cook. So this wasn't the end for me. I started a process of trial and error to find out what my body could tolerate – and what my body wouldn't tolerate. I simply took the dishes that I had liked before my surgery and changed them. Mostly, I cut high-fat ingredients and tried to find substitutes. Also, I tested how much fat my body could tolerate in one meal, and I adapted my recipes to that. Now I have a small collection of recipes tailor-made for people who had their gallbladder removed.

Have fun and a good time when trying my recipes. I would love to hear from you what you think about my recipes – in a review or via e-mail.

To a healthy, low-fat diet.

Iris Pilzer

THE WAY OF LIFE WITHOUT A GALLBLADDER

Eat a lot of fibers. They prevent your body from forming new gallstones. You can find lots of fibers in oatmeal, most vegetables, crispbread and bread made from rye flour.

Eat 5 to 6 small meals a day to make things easier for your digestive system.

Try to find out how much fat your body can tolerate in one meal. Then try to eat exactly this amount of fat at each meal.

Don't worry if your meal has more fat than your body can stomach: take an artichoke capsule or drink a beer with your meal (preferably non- alcoholic beer).

Find out which foods your body can't tolerate. Try to steer clear of these foods in the future. Carefully try foods that cause bloating, such as onions, garlic, legumes, cabbage and kale, cucumbers, and peppers and chilis (including paprika). Spicy dishes might cause your digestive system to rebel.

When you eat out: Ask what's in what you want to order. If you can't tolerate some types of foods, tell them. There's no need to suffer so that others have less work (for which you still have to pay) or aren't offended.

Drink a lot of liquid. Best would be water and tea without sugar. Aim to drink 7 to 9 cups of liquid a day. And while you're at it, test if you can tolerate carbonated water.

Buy day-old bread. If you can't get hold of any, toast fresh bread for 5 seconds. You might also have a problem with other freshly baked pastries (e.g., yeast dough).

Avoid processed foods. These are often heavily spiced. Fresh food is better for your digestion (and it tastes better!).

Reduce your alcohol intake. Your liver will thank you!

Keep a food log so that you don't lose track of what you should and what you shouldn't eat.

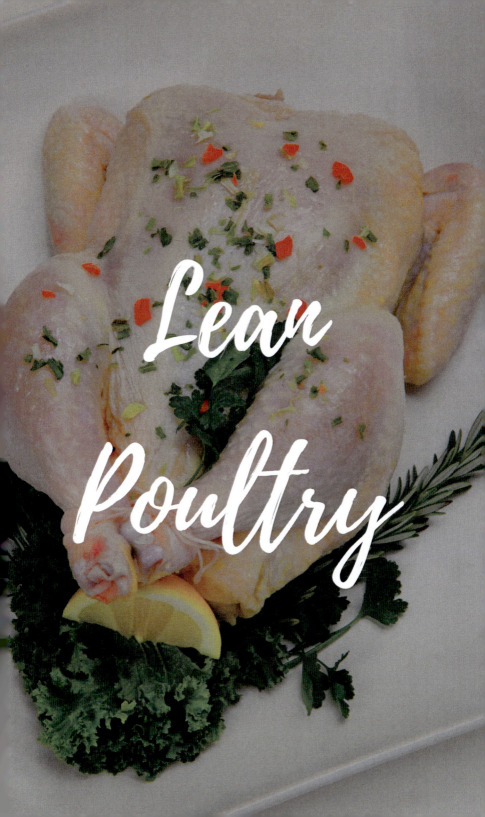

Caesar's Salad with Chicken

For 2 servings:
2 slices of bread • ½ tbsp butter • 2 small chicken breast fillets • 1 tbsp olive oil • 1 green salad • 1 small clove of garlic • 1 oz cream • 3 ½ oz mayonnaise • 1 tbsp grated Parmesan cheese • ½ tbsp white wine vinegar • salt, pepper • a handful shaved Parmesan cheese

- Cut the bread into small cubes. Heat the butter in a medium-size pan. Add the bread cubes and stir-fry until golden. Remove the bread cubes from the can and place on paper towels.
- Wash the chicken breast fillets, pat dry and cut into bite-size pieces. Heat 2 tbsp of olive oil in a pan. Stir-fry the chicken for 5 minutes until well done.
- Wash the salad, shake dry and cut into bite-size pieces.
- For the dressing: peel the garlic and place in a blender. Add the mayonnaise, the cream, the parmesan, the vinegar, salt and pepper and blend until smooth.
- Place the salad and the chicken in a large bowl. Carefully toss and serve with croutons and parmesan.

Salad with Chicken Breast

For 1 serving:
1 small chicken breast fillet • 1 tbsp soy sauce • ½ tspn honey • pepper • 1 small carrot • 1 spring onion • 3 ½ oz cherry tomatoes • 7 oz green salad • 2 tbsp vinegar • sugar • 4 tbsp olive oil

- Wash the chicken breast fillets, pat dry and cut into bite-size pieces. In a bowl, mix the soy sauce, the honey and a pinch of pepper. Add the chicken and marinate for 20 to 30 minutes.
- Peel the carrot and cut into thin strips. Wash the spring onions and cut into rings. Wash and halve the cherry tomatoes. Wash the salad, shake dry and cut into bite-size pieces. Place the greens in a large bowl.
- Heat 1 tbsp of olive oil in a small pan. Add the chicken pieces and stir-fry for 5 minutes until well done.
- In the meantime, mix the vinegar with the salt, pepper, sugar and oil. Pour the dressing on the salad and toss well.
- Add some salt to the chicken. Place the chicken on the salad. Serve hot.

Tip: If you're in a hurry, use salad from a bag.

CHICKEN SKEWERS IN PEANUT SAUCE

For 2 servings:
5 ½ oz basmati rice • ½ clove of garlic • 1 cm ginger • 1 small red chili • 2 tbsp peanut creme (or peanut butter) • 1 tspn soy sauce • 1 lime • 2 chicken breast fillets • honey

- Preheat the oven to 440 °F.
- Bring 10 fl oz of water to the boil in a small pot. Once boiling, add salt and the rice. Let the rice cook for 10 minutes at low heat, then remove it from the heat and let it rest for another 10 minutes.
- In the meantime, peel the garlic and the ginger and finely chop. Wash and deseed the chili and finely chop.
- Squeeze the lime juice into a bowl. Add the peanut crème and the diced vegetables. Mix well. Add a little water if the sauce is not smooth.
- Wash the chicken breast fillets, pat dry and cut into bite-size pieces. Place the chicken on skewers. Slice cross-wise on both sides. Place the skewers in a baking dish. Place the peanut sauce on top and rub into the chicken. Bake in the oven for 8 to 10 minutes.
- Serve hot with rice.

CHICKEN WITH STEWED VEGETABLES

For 2 servings:
1 lb frozen green vegetables • 2 chicken breast fillets • salt, pepper • rosemary • 1 tbsp olive oil • 4 slices of bacon

- Prepare the vegetables according to the instructions on the packaging.
- Wash the chicken breast fillets and pat dry. Season well with salt, pepper and rosemary. Place the chicken in a freezer bag and flatten with a rolling pin.
- Heat the olive oil in a pan. Add the chicken breasts and fry until golden and cooked through. Turn the chicken breasts after 3 to 4 minutes.
- In the meantime, cut the bacon into thin strips. Add to the chicken breasts and stir-fry.
- Season the vegetables with salt and pepper. Serve hot with the chicken breasts.

Chicken ragout with tomatoes

For 2 servings:

2 cloves of garlic • 1 onion • 1 small chili • ½ lb cherry tomatoes • thyme • 1 tbsp olive oil • 2 tspn turmeric • ½ tbsp brown sugar • 2 tbsp red wine vinegar • 1 organic lemon • 11 oz chicken breast • salt, pepper • 1 bag boil-in-the-bag rice

- Peel the onion and the garlic and finely chop. Deseed the chili, wash and finely chop. Wash the cherry tomatoes.
- Heat the olive oil in a pot. Add the onion, garlic and chili and stir-fry until soft. Season with turmeric and thyme. Add the tomatoes. Sprinkle the sugar on top. Add the red wine vinegar and 5 fl oz of water. Stir well. Place the lid on the pot and cook on low heat for 15 minutes.
- Wash the lemon with hot water and cut into slices. Wash the chicken breasts, pat dry and cut into bite-size pieces. Place the lemon and the chicken in the pot. Season with salt and pepper. Place the lid on the pot and cook on low heat for another 15 minutes.
- In der meantime, prepare the rice according to the instructions on the packaging. Serve the ragout hot with rice.

Chicken ragout Ohio

For 2 servings:

2 onions • 1 clove of garlic • 2 tbsp olive oil • salt, pepper • 1 bell pepper • ½ can (7 oz) white beans • ½ can (5 oz) sweet corn • 2 oz breadcrumbs • cayenne pepper • 2 tomatoes • ½ roasted chicken • 5 ½ oz peas (frozen)

- Peel the onions and the garlic and finely chop.
- Heat the olive oil in a large pot. Add the onions and garlic and fry until soft. Season well with salt and pepper. Add 2 cups of water, place the lid on top and cook for 10 minutes.
- Deseed the bell pepper, wash and cut into strips. Drain and rinse the beans and the corn. Add the vegetables to the ragout and stir well.
- Add the breadcrumbs and season to taste with cayenne pepper. Wash the tomatoes and roughly chop. Remove the bones from the chicken. Place the chicken and the tomatoes in the pot.
- Cook the ragout on low heat for 10 minutes. Serve hot.

FARFALLE WITH CHICKEN AND TOMATOES

For 2 servings:
7 oz farfalle • 2 small chicken breasts • salt, pepper • 2 tbsp olive oil • 1 can (15 oz) cherry tomatoes (or 1 can of peeled tomatoes) • ½ tbsp sugar • 2 handfuls of grated Pecorino cheese

- Prepare the farfalle according to the instructions on the packaging.
- Wash the chicken breasts, pat dry and season well with salt and pepper. Place the chicken in a freezer bag and flatten with a rolling pin.
- Heat 2 tbsp of olive oil in a medium-size pan. Add the chicken breasts and fry until golden and cooked through. Turn the chicken breasts after 3 to 4 minutes. Remove the chicken breasts from the pan and cut into strips.
- Sprinkle the sugar into the pan and leave it to caramelize. Add the canned tomatoes (careful, the caramel is hot!) and stir carefully. Season with salt, pepper and a handful of Pecorino cheese and stir well.
- Serve the farfalle with chicken strips, tomato sauce and Pecorino.

TURKEY WRAPS

For 4 wraps:
3 ½ oz turkey ham in slices • 3 ½ oz Emmental cheese in slices • ½ small iceberg lettuce • 4 oz red grapes • ½ can (4 oz) tangerines • 4 oz yoghurt • 3 tbsp mayonnaise • ½ tspn curry powder • 2 tbsp chopped walnuts • salt, pepper • 4 tortillas

- Cut the turkey ham and the cheese into strips. Cut the salad into strips, wash and shake dry. Wash and halve the grapes. Drain the tangerines while retaining the liquid from the can. Roughly chop the walnuts.
- For the sauce: mix the yoghurt, the mayonnaise, the curry powder, the walnuts and 4 tbsp of tangerine juice. Season well with salt and pepper.
- Prepare the tortillas according to the instructions on the packaging.
- Spread 1 tspn of sauce on a tortilla. Place the iceberg lettuce, tangerines and grapes on top. Place the turkey ham and cheese strips in the middle of the tortilla. Sprinkle with a little sauce, wrap and enjoy.

Glass noodle salad with chicken breast

For 2 servings:

9 oz chicken breast • 1 tbsp soy sauce • 3 oz glass noodles • 1 small red chili • 1 clove of garlic • 13 oz carrots • 10 oz leek • 1 tbsp oil • salt, pepper • ¼ tspn ground ginger • juice of 1 lime

- Wash the chicken breast, pat dry and cut into bite-size pieces. Marinate in a small bowl with soy sauce.
- Prepare the glass noodles according to the instructions on the packaging. Then chill with cold water and cut into shorter pieces.
- Halve the chili, deseed, wash and cut into thin strips. Peel the garlic and finely chop. Peel the carrots and thinly slice. Wash the leek and cut into rings.
- Heat the oil in a pan. Stir-fry the chicken for 5 to 7 minutes until golden and cooked through. Remove the chicken from the pan, season with salt and pepper and set aside.
- Stir-fry the garlic, carrots, chili and leek in the hot pan. Remove from the pan and let get cold.
- Place everything in a bowl. Season well with salt, pepper, ginger and lime juice and stir well.

Kentucky salad

For 2 servings:

½ head of lettuce • 2 tbsp berries (you can use thawed frozen berries) • ½ grapefruit • 2 tbsp raspberry vinegar • salt, pepper • 5 tbsp olive oil • 5 ½ oz turkey breast

- Wash the salad and cut into bite-size pieces. Wash the berries.
- Cut the top and bottom off the grapefruit. Carefully cut away the skin. Then cut the grapefruit into segments. Carefully mix with the salad.
- For the dressing: mix vinegar, salt, pepper and 3 tbsp of oil. Pour over the salad and toss well.
- Wash the turkey breast, pat dry and cut into strips.
- Heat the remaining oil in a pan. Fry the turkey strips for 5 to 7 minutes until golden and cooked through. Season with salt and pepper.
- Place the turkey on top of the salad and serve immediately.

Crispy Pork

Mini pork skewers

For 6 skewers:

½ lb pork • 3 tbsp olive oil • 1 organic lemon • 2 cloves of garlic • ½ bunch parsley • ½ tbsp Ras-el-Hanout (spice blend) • salt, pepper

- Wash the pork, pat dry and cut into bite-size pieces. Place the pork pieces in a flat bowl.
- Using the garlic press, add the garlic to the pork. Wash the parsley, shake dry, finely chop and add to the pork. Add oil and spices and mix well.
- Place the pork in the refrigerator to marinate for at least 2 hours.
- Water wooden skewers for 30 minutes. Place the pork pieces on the skewers.
- Heat a griddle pan. Fry the skewers until they are golden. Turn a few times and use the rest of the marinade when turning.

Bean & ham salad

For 2 servings:

1 can (15 oz) beans • 5 ½ ham (raw or cooked) • ½ cup sour cream • 1 tbsp yoghurt • 1 tbsp vinegar • ½ tbsp Worcestershire sauce • salt, pepper, sweet paprika • 1 tbsp chopped chive (frozen)

- Drain the beans and rinse until the foam disappears. Cut the ham into strips.
- For the dressing: mix the sour cream with the yoghurt, the vinegar and the Worcestershire sauce. Season with salt, pepper and sweet paprika.
- Place everything in a bowl and toss well. Let the salad rest a little.
- Garnish the salad with a pinch of sweet paprika and the chopped chive before serving.

Eggplant Pan

For 2 servings:

3 tbsp oil • 4 slices of bacon • 1 lb eggplant • garlic powder, salt, pepper • ½ lb tomatoes • 6 sausages

- Cut the bacon into fine strips. Heat a griddle pan and fry the bacon.
- Wash the eggplant and cut into slices. Add 2 tbsp of oil and the eggplant to the pan and fry on medium heat. Season with garlic powder, salt and pepper. Put on the lid and cook on low heat for 15 minutes.
- Wash the tomatoes, cut into quarters, remove the stem and roughly chop. Add to the eggplant and cook on low heat for 10 minutes.
- In the meantime, heat 1 tbsp of oil in a second pan. Fry the sausages until done. Serve hot with the vegetables.

Tips: Instead of garlic powder, you can also use a clove of garlic. This dish will also taste great with mushrooms, zucchini or bell peppers.

Ground Meat with Beans

For 2 servings:

½ lb tomatoes • 2 onions • 1 clove of garlic • 2 tbsp olive oil • ½ lb ground meat (pork or mixed) • 1 can (15 oz) white beans • salt, pepper • cayenne pepper, marjoram

- Wash the tomatoes and roughly chop. Don't forget to remove the stems.
- Peel the onions and the garlic and finely chop.
- Heat the oil in a pan. Add the onion and the garlic and fry until soft. Add the ground meat and fry until it has a nice brown color.
- Add the tomatoes and the beans directly from the can. Season well with salt, pepper, a pinch of cayenne pepper and marjoram to taste. Cook on low heat for 10 minutes.

LASAGNA

For 2 servings:
4 slices of bacon • 1 tbsp olive oil • 1 large onion • 2 cloves of garlic • 1 can (15 oz) peeled tomatoes • 2 tbsp dried pizza herbs (oregano, thyme, rosemary) • salt, pepper, sugar • ½ lb ground meat • dried oregano • 3 tbsp butter • 2 tbsp flour • 17 fl oz milk • nutmeg • lasagna sheets • 2 oz grated Parmesan cheese

- Cut the bacon into fine strips. Heat a medium-size pan and fry the bacon.
- Peel the onion and the garlic and finely chop. Add the olive oil to the bacon. Add the onion and the garlic and fry until soft.
- Add the tomatoes. Crush larger pieces with a wooden spoon. Add the herbs and the salt, pepper and sugar. Stir well and cook on low heat.
- In the meantime, heat a second pan. Add the ground meat and stir-fry until it has a nice brown color. Season well with oregano, salt and pepper. Add the tomato sauce, stir well and cook on low heat for 15 minutes.
- Preheat the oven to 400 °F.
- For the béchamel sauce: heat 2 tbsp of butter in a large pot. When the butter has melted, reduce the heat and stir in the flour.
- When the flour starts to burn, remove the pot from the stove. Add half of the milk and whisk with a wire whisk. Place the pot back on the stove and turn up the heat. When the sauce starts to thicken, add a little milk and stir well. Repeat this until all of the milk is gone. Remove the pot from the stove. Season well with nutmeg, salt and pepper.
- Grease a baking dish with 1 tbsp of butter. Spoon a third of the tomato sauce into the baking dish and add a layer of lasagna sheets. Then spoon a third of the béchamel sauce on top and, again, add a layer of lasagna sheets. Repeat twice more until you finish with a layer of béchamel sauce. Sprinkle the grated Parmesan on top. Bake in the oven for 30 minutes.

Tip: This dish is elaborate to prepare, but you can easily double the ingredients and freeze the rest. I always use baking dishes that are large enough for 1 or 2 servings. When the tomato sauce and the béchamel sauce layers have cooled, I put on a lid and place it in the freezer. If I'm in the mood for lasagna, I let it thaw overnight in the fridge and bake it as usual in the oven for 30 minutes.

Pasta with Ham and Peas

For 2 servings:

7 oz tagliatelle • 1 small onion • 1 tbsp butter • 8 oz cream • 5 ½ oz cooked ham • 7 oz peas (frozen) • ½ stock cube (meat broth) • 2 oz grated Parmesan cheese • salt, pepper

- Prepare the pasta according to the instructions on the packaging.
- Peel the onion and finely chop.
- Heat the butter in a pan. Add the onion and stir-fry until soft. Add the cream and reduce the heat to low heat. Bring the cream to a boil.
- In the meantime, cut the ham into strips. Add the ham and the peas to the cream. Crumble the stock cube into the pan. Stir well and cook on low heat for 10 minutes.
- Stir the Parmesan cheese into the sauce. Season well with salt and pepper and serve hot.

Fried Chorizo with Herbs

For 2 servings:

2 cloves of garlic • ¾ lb chorizo • 2 tbsp olive oil • 4 tbsp herbs (frozen or fresh) • baguette

- Peel the garlic and finely chop. Cut the chorizo into 5 mm slices.
- Heat a pan. Add the chorizo slices and stir-fry on medium heat until crisp.
- Remove the chorizo from the pan and place on paper towels. Pour the fat out of the pan and wipe with paper towels.
- Heat the olive oil in the pan. Stir-fry the garlic for 30 seconds. Reduce the heat and add the herbs. Fry for 1 to 2 minutes. Add the chorizo slices and heat while stirring.
- Serve hot with baguette.

GROUND MEAT WITH SOYBEAN SPROUTS

For 2 servings:
1 bag boil-in-the-bag rice (4 ½ oz) • 1 tbsp peanut oil • 1 onion • 11 oz ground beef • pepper • 4 tbsp soy sauce • 7 oz soybean sprouts (from the can)

- Prepare the rice according to the instructions on the packaging.
- Peel the onion and finely chop.
- Heat the oil in a pan. Add the onion and stir-fry until soft. Add the ground meat. Break the meat up with a wooden spoon and fry until it has a nice brown color. Season with pepper and soy sauce.
- Drain the soybean sprouts and add to the meat. Heat briefly so that the soybean sprouts stay crunchy.
- Serve the meat together with the rice.

ONIONS ON GROUND BEEF

For 2 servings:
3 tbsp olive oil • 14 oz small onions • 1 can (15 oz) peeled tomatoes • 4 ½ oz ground beef • salt, pepper, thyme

- Peel the onions.
- Heat 1 tbsp of olive oil in a pot. Stir-fry the onions.
- Add the tomatoes, break them up with a wooden spoon and stir well. Cook on low heat for 15 minutes.
- In the meantime, heat the remaining oil in a second pan. Add the ground beef and stir-fry until it has a nice brown color.
- Season both the ground beef and the vegetables with salt, pepper and thyme.
- Spread the ground beef on 2 plates. Add the tomatoes and onions on top and serve hot.

Steak Sandwich

For 2 servings:
10 oz sirloin steak • salt, pepper • thyme • 2 tbsp rapeseed oil • 1 ciabatta bread or baguette • 2 red onions • sugar • ¼ cucumber • 1 ½ mayonnaise • wasabi paste • 1 tspn vinegar • 7 oz rocket (from the bag)

- Wash the steak and pat dry. Season well with salt, pepper and thyme. Heat 1 tbsp of oil in a pan. Fry the steak (each side 1 to 2 minutes for well done, 2 to 3 minutes for medium and 3 to 4 minutes for well done). Remove the steak from the pan, wrap it in aluminum foil and set aside.
- Peel the onions, cut in halves and then into strips. Heat 1 tbsp of oil in a pan. Stir-fry the onion for 5 minutes. Then add 1 tspn of sugar, salt and pepper and leave it to caramelize. Remove from the stove.
- Wash the rocket and shake dry. Wash the cucumber, peel it if you want and cut into slices. In a small bowl, mix some wasabi-paste (hot!), mayonnaise, vinegar, salt and 1 pinch of sugar.
- Cut the bread open lengthwise. Remove the steak from the foil and cut into strips. Spread the wasabi mayonnaise on the bread. Place the onions, a little rocket and the steak on top. Spread some wasabi mayonnaise on the upper half of the bread and place on top.

Avocado & Steak Pan

For 2 servings:
1 lb cherry tomatoes • 1 onion • ½ bunch parsley • 1 avocado • 1 lime • ½ lb steak • 2 tbsp olive oil • salt, pepper

- Wash the tomatoes and cut into halves. Peel the onion and roughly chop. Wash the parsley, shake dry and roughly chop. Halve the avocado, remove the core and the peel, roughly chop and sprinkle with lime juice.
- Wash the steak, pat dry and cut in to broad strips. Heat the oil in a pan. Stir-fry the steak strips for 2 minutes on all sides. Season well with salt and pepper. Remove the steak strips from the pan, wrap it in aluminum foil and set aside.
- Add the onion to the hot pan and stir-fry until soft. Add the tomatoes and stir-fry for 2 to 3 minutes. Add the steak and the avocado and heat until they are hot. Season with salt and pepper and sprinkle with parsley. Serve hot.

Meat balls with strawberry salsa

For 2 servings:
4 oz strawberries • 1 small chili • 1 small onion • juice of ½ lime •
1 tbsp honey • salt, pepper • 1 mozzarella • 10 oz ground beef • 1 egg •
2 tbsp olive oil • a handful cherry tomatoes

- For the salsa: wash the strawberries. Deseed the chili, wash and roughly chop. Peel the onion and finely chop.
- Place the strawberries, the chili, a quarter of the onion, lime juice, honey, salt and pepper in a blender and roughly blend. Fill the salsa in a bowl and put in the fridge.
- Drain the mozzarella and roughly chop.
- Knead the round meat with the egg, the rest of the onion and salt and pepper. Form 12 meat balls and press flat. Place the mozzarella pieces in the middle of each meat circle. Close the meat above the mozzarella and form a ball.
- Heat the oil in a pan. Add the meat balls and stir-fry on low to medium heat for 20 minutes, turning regularly.
- In the meantime, wash the tomatoes and add them to the meat balls after 15 minutes. Serve hot with strawberry salsa.

Meat & tomato pot with spinach

For 2 servings:
2 onion • 2 cloves of garlic • 2 tspn olive oil • ½ lb ground beef •
2 tspn tomato puree • 1 can (15 oz) peeled tomatoes • 11 oz spinach (frozen) •
salt, pepper • 3 oz feta

- Peel the onions and the cloves of garlic and finely chop.
- Heat the oil in a pan. Add the onion and the garlic and fry until soft. Add the ground beef and the tomato puree and stir-fry until the beef has a nice brown color.
- Add the peeled tomatoes and the spinach. Season with salt and pepper. Put on the lid and cook for 10 minutes on low to medium heat. Stir regularly.
- After 10 minutes, season again with salt and pepper. Serve hot with feta crumbled on top.

Steak Wraps with Salsa and Guacamole

For 4 wraps:
4 tortillas • 10 oz ground beef • 1 tbsp olive oil • salt, pepper • 1 lettuce heart • 2 tomatoes • 4 tbsp sweet corn (from the can) • 1 oz grated cheese

- Heat the oil in a pan. Add the ground beef and stir-fry until the beef has a nice brown color. Season with salt and pepper and keep warm.
- In the meantime, cut the salad into fine strips, wash and shake dry. Wash the tomatoes and roughly chop (don't forget to remove the stem).
- Prepare the tortillas according to the instructions on the packaging.
- Place a tortilla on a plate. Spread a little guacamole on the tortilla. Place the salad, tomatoes, sweet corn, cheese and beef on top. Sprinkle with salsa. Wrap up and enjoy with salsa.

For the salsa:
1 onion • 2 cloves of garlic • 1 chili • 1 tbsp olive oil • 1 can (15 oz) canned tomatoes • 2 tbsp white wine vinegar • ½ tspn sugar • salt, pepper

- Peel the onion and the garlic and finely chop. Deseed the chili, wash and finely chop.
- Heat the oil in a small pot. Add the onion and garlic and fry for 2 minutes. Add the chili and fry for 1 minute. Add the tomatoes and break them up with a wooden spoon. Cook on low heat for 5 minutes.
- Roughly blend (if you want) and season well with white wine vinegar, sugar, salt and pepper.

For the guacamole:
1 ripe (soft) avocado • 2 spring onions • 2 tbsp sour cream • juice of ½ lime • ¼ tspn ground cumin • salt, pepper

- Wash the avocado, halve and remove the core. Press the flesh from the peel with your fingers and crush with a fork.
- Wash the spring onions and cut into finger-size pieces. Cut the pieces lengthwise into quarters and finely chop.
- Add the sour cream, the lime juice, the cumin and the spring onion. Stir well and season to taste with salt and pepper.

Tip: Try the wraps with steak strips instead of ground beef!

Glass Noodles with Steak

For 2 servings:
3 ½ oz glass noodles • 2 cloves of garlic • 2 tbsp soy sauce • 7 oz steak • ½ cucumber • 1 red onion • 1 oz peanuts • 2 limes • chili flakes • ½ tbsp brown sugar or cane sugar • salt • 2 tbsp sesame oil • 1 tbsp peanut oil

- Prepare the glass noodles according to the instructions on the packaging. Then chill with cold water, drain and cut into shorter pieces.
- Peel the garlic and finely chop. Mix with soy sauce. Wash the steak, pat dry and cut into strips. Place the steak strips in the marinade.
- Peel the cucumber, cut in halve lengthwise, remove the seeds and cut into strips. Peel the onion and roughly chop.
- Roast the peanuts in a pan until they start to burn.
- For the dressing: mix the juice of 1 ½ limes, the chili flakes, sugar, salt and the sesame oil. Place the glass noodles, the cucumber, the onion and the dressing in a bowl and toss well.
- Heat the peanut oil in a pan. Stir-fry the steak strips for 3 to 4 minutes. Place on the salad and garnish with pieces of lime.

Zucchini Noodles with Ground Beef

For 2 servings:
2 large zucchini • 1 onion • ½ lb ground beef • 1 tbsp olive oil • salt, pepper • 2 tbsp tomato puree • 1 tbsp flour • 7 fl oz vegetable stock • ½ bunch basil • 1 ½ oz shaved Grana Padano cheese

- Wash the zucchini and cut into "noodles" with a speed peeler. Peel the onion and cut into strips.
- Heat a pan. Add the ground beef and stir-fry without fat until it has a nice brown color. Add the oil and stir well. Add the vegetables and stir-fry for 3 to 4 minutes.
- Add the tomato puree and stir well. Add the flour and fry for 1 to 2 minutes. Pour in the vegetable stock and cook for 8 minutes or until the vegetables are soft.
- In the meantime, wash the basil and shake dry. Remove the leaves and roughly chop.
- Place the vegetables and the round beef on a plate. Sprinkle with basil and cheese. Serve hot.

PASTA SALAD WITH SEAFOOD

For 2 servings:
7 oz short pasta • 1 lb seafood (frozen) • 3 ½ oz mayonnaise • 2 tbsp chopped parsley (frozen) • cayenne pepper • 1 tspn lemon juice • 4 red radishes • 1 small red bell pepper • salt, pepper

- Prepare the pasta and the seafood according to the instructions on the packaging. Chill both afterwards.
- For the dressing: Place the mayonnaise, the parsley, the cayenne pepper and the lemon juice in a large bowl and stir well.
- Wash the red radishes and cut into thin slices. Deseed the bell peppers, wash and cut into thin strips.
- Add the pasta, the seafood, the red radishes and the bell peppers to the dressing. Toss carefully. Season with salt and pepper before serving.

PASTA CASSEROLE WITH SEAFOOD

For 2 servings:
6 oz short pasta • ½ lb seafood (frozen) • 1 onion • 2 cloves of garlic • 1 tbsp olive oil • 1 can (15 oz) canned tomatoes • 2 fl oz white wine (to taste) • 1 tbsp chopped basil • 1 tbsp chopped parsley • salt, pepper • 1 pinch of sugar • butter

- Prepare the pasta and the seafood according to the instructions on the packaging.
- Preheat the oven to 400 °F.
- Peel the onion and the garlic and finely chop.
- Heat the oil in a pan. Add the onion and the garlic and stir-fry until soft. Add the canned tomatoes and break them up with a wooden spoon. Pour in the white wine, place the lid on the pot and cook on low heat for 10 minutes.
- Add the basil, the parsley, salt, pepper and sugar and stir well. Remove the pan from the stove and add the seafood. Stir carefully.
- Grease a casserole dish with butter. Mix the pasta and the sauce carefully and place in the casserole dish. Cover with aluminum foil and bake in the oven for 20 minutes.

Salad with Calamari

For 2 servings:
14 oz ready-to-cook calamari (let thaw if frozen) • 4 tbsp olive oil • 2 tbsp lemon juice • 1 clove of garlic • 2 tbsp chopped parsley (frozen) • 1 tbsp dried marjoram • 1 pinch of cayenne pepper • 1 small zucchini • 4 oz rocket • ½ lb cherry tomatoes

- Cut the calamari into broad rings.
- Heat 2 tbsp of olive oil in a pan. Fry the calamari rings for 3 minutes. Remove from the pan and place in a bowl.
- Add 2 tbsp of olive oil, lemon juice, parsley, marjoram and cayenne pepper. Using a garlic press, add the garlic. Stir carefully and place in the fridge. Marinate for 2 to 8 hours.
- For the salad: Wash the zucchini and cut into "noodles" with a speed peeler. Wash the rocket and the tomatoes. Place everything in a large bowl. Add the calamari rings with the marinade. Stir well and enjoy.

Tip: If you can't get any calamari, you can use a seafood mix instead.

Garlic Shrimps

For 2 servings:
3 cloves of garlic • parsley • ½ lemon • 3 tbsp olive oil • 14 oz frozen cooked shrimps (thawed) • chili flakes • salt, pepper • baguette

- Peel the garlic and cut into fine slices. Wash the parsley, shake dry and finely chop. Wash the lemon and cut into quarters.
- Heat the oil in a pan on small heat. Add the garlic and the chili flakes and stir-fry for 1 minute. Add the shrimps and stir-fry for 2 to 3 minutes until the shrimps are hot.
- Switch off the stove. Add the parsley and stir carefully. Season with salt and pepper.
- Serve the shrimps hot with lemon and baguette.

Puff Pastry with Shrimp Filling

For 2 servings:
1 package puff pastry • 7 oz shrimps in brine • 1 hard-boiled egg • 1 tbsp sweet paprika • 1 pinch of cayenne pepper • 1 tbsp chopped parsley (frozen)

- Preheat the oven to 440 °F.
- Heat the butter in a pot. When the butter has melted, reduce the temperature and stir in the flour. Remove the pot from the stove when the flour is golden. Stir in half of the milk with a wire whisk.
- Place the pot back on the stove and turn on the heat. When the liquid starts to thicken, add some milk and stir well. Repeat until the milk is one. Season with nutmeg, salt and pepper.
- Drain the shrimps and add to the sauce. Peel the egg, roughly chop and add to the sauce. Season with sweet paprika, cayenne pepper and parsley. Stir well.
- Roll out the puff pastry dough and cut into small squares. Place a little sauce on every piece. Spread a little water on the edges. Fold the dough into triangles and press the edges with your fingers
- Bake in the oven for 15 to 20 minutes.

Shrimp & Vegetable Salad

For 2 servings:
4 ½ oz cooked shrimps • 2 large tomatoes • 1 yellow bell pepper • 1 clove of garlic • 2 spring onions • 1 lime • 3 tbsp olive oil • salt, pepper, sugar, chili powder • baguette

- Drain the shrimps (or thaw if frozen).
- For the dressing: in a large bowl, mix the oil with the juice of ½ lime, salt, pepper, sugar and chili powder. Add the shrimps and marinate for 15 minutes.
- Wash the tomatoes, cut in halve, remove the stem and roughly chop. Deseed the bell pepper, wash and chop. Peel the garlic. Wash the spring onion and cut into rings. Cut the second half of the lime into slices.
- Add the vegetables to the shrimps and stir carefully. Using a garlic press, add the garlic. Add salt and pepper if necessary. Garnish with lime slices and serve with baguette.

Shrimp & melon wraps

For 4 wraps:
½ small iceberg lettuce • ½ cucumber • ½ Galia melon or Cantaloupe • 3 ½ oz mayonnaise • 3 ½ oz sour cream • 2 tbsp ketchup • 1 tbsp tomato puree • 1 tbsp lemon juice • salt, pepper • 14 oz shrimps in brine • 4 tortillas

- Cut the lettuce into strips, wash and shake dry. Wash the cucumber, peel and cut into strips lengthwise. Halve the melon, remove the seeds and the peel and cut into thin slices.
- For the sauce: mix the mayonnaise with the sour cream, the ketchup, the tomato puree and the lemon juice. Season with salt and pepper.
- Drain the shrimps. Stir in carefully.
- Prepare the tortillas according to the instructions on the packaging.
- Spread the lettuce on the tortilla. Spread the sauce on top. Add the cucumber sticks and the melon slices in the middle. Wrap and enjoy.

Tip: The next day, prepare a delicious salad from the leftover lettuce, cucumber and melon. Add a little yoghurt dressing and enjoy!

Vegetable noodles with shrimps

For 2 servings:
1 zucchini • 1 carrot • 5 oz cherry tomatoes • 1 small cucumber • 1 bunch of herbs • 1 clove of garlic • 5 oz shrimps in brine • 4 tbsp olive oil • salt, pepper • 1 tbsp mustard • 1 tbsp honey • 4 tbsp vinegar • baguette

- Wash the zucchini. Peel the carrot. Using a speed peeler, cut into thin strips. Place in a bowl with water.
- Wash the tomatoes and cut into half. Peel the cucumber and slice. Wash the herbs and shake dry. Chop the leaves. Peel the garlic and cut into fine slices. Drain the shrimps.
- Heat 2 tbsp of olive oil in a pan. Stir-fry the garlic for 30 seconds. Add the shrimps and stir-fry for 30 seconds. Remove both from the pan.
- For the dressing: Mix the mustard with the honey, and vinegar. Season well with salt and pepper and add the oil little by little.
- Drain the vegetable strips. Place in a large bowl. Add the tomatoes, the herbs, the cucumber slices and the dressing. Place the shrimps on top and serve warm with baguette.

Warm Tomato Salad with Salmon

For 2 servings:
1 organic lemon • 2 salmon filets (let thaw if frozen) • 2 tbsp olive oil • 1 tbsp honey • chili flakes • 2 tbsp soy sauce • pepper • 7 oz cherry tomatoes • 1 celery stem • 1 clove of garlic • 2 tbsp olive oil • salt, pepper • 2 tbsp vinegar • 2 oz pitted black olives

- Preheat the oven to 400 °F.
- Wash the lemon with hot water, dry off and cut into slices. Spread in a baking dish.
- Wash the salmon, pat dry and place on the lemon slices. In a small bowl, mix the olive oil with the honey, chili flakes, soy sauce and pepper. Spread the marinade on the salmon and place in the oven for 10 minutes.
- In the meantime, wash the cherry tomatoes and cut into half. Wash the celery and finely slice. Roughly chop the celery greens. Peel the garlic and cut into fine slices.
- Heat the remaining olive oil in a pan. Stir-fry the garlic, the tomatoes and the celery for 3 to 4 minutes. Season with salt, pepper and vinegar. Place on two plates. Add the olives and place the salmon on top. Serve hot.

Smoked Salmon Wraps

For 4 wraps:
1 small oak leaf lettuce (or romaine lettuce) • ½ cucumber • 2 spring onions • 2 tbsp Dijon mustard • 2 tbsp honey • 2 tbsp vinegar • 1 tbsp sunflower oil • 1 tspn dried dill • salt, pepper • 8 slices of smoked salmon • 4 tortillas

- Wash the lettuce, shake dry and roughly chop. Peel the cucumber, cut into finger-size pieces and then into sticks. Wash the spring onions and cut into rings.
- In a small bowl, mix the mustard and the honey. Add the vinegar and stir well. Add the oil little by little. Season with dill, salt and pepper and stir well.
- Prepare the tortillas according to the instructions on the packaging.
- Place 2 pieces of salmon on a tortilla. Spread the lettuce on top. Sprinkle with the sauce. Place the cucumber sticks in the middle of the tortilla. Sprinkle with spring onion rings, wrap and enjoy.

Asian Salmon with Sprout Salad

For 2 servings:
1 inch ginger • 2 cloves of garlic • 1 small red onion • pepper • olive oil • chili flakes • 1 tbsp soy sauce • 1 lime • 2 frozen salmon fillets (thawed) • five-spice powder • 1 lb sprouts (fresh or canned) • 2 oz cashews (to taste) • honey • 1 tspn sesame oil

- Preheat the oven to 400 °F.
- Peel the ginger, the garlic and the onion and finely chop Place in a small baking dish and season with salt, pepper. Sprinkle with olive oil.
- Wash the salmon and pat dry. Place the salmon in the baking dish skin up. Sprinkle with the juice of ½ lime and with chili flakes. Sprinkle with olive oil and season with five-spice powder. Place in the oven for 15 to 20 minutes.
- For the salad: wash or drain the sprouts. Place the cashews in a freezer bag and crush with a meat tenderizer (or something similar).
- Heat a small pan. Fry the cashews on small heat until they start to burn. Remove the pan from the stove, sprinkle with honey, stir and set aside.
- Place the sprouts in a bowl. Season well with chili flakes, soy sauce, 1 tbsp of olive oil, sesame oil and the juice of ½ lime. Stir well and sprinkle with cashews. Serve with the salmon.

Salad with Salmon Cubes

For 2 servings:
½ lb green salad • 5 ½ lb cherry tomatoes • 1 cucumber • 10 oz salmon fillet • salt, pepper • 3 tbsp olive oil • 2 tbsp vinegar • 1 tbsp mustard • 1 tbsp honey

- Preheat the oven to 400 °F.
- Wash the salmon, pat dry and cut into cubes. Remove the skin in the process. Season with salt and pepper. Spread 1 tbsp of oil in a small baking dish. Place the salmon in the baking dish and bake in the oven for 5 to 10 minutes.
- In the meantime, wash the salad and shake dry. Wash the tomatoes and cut into half. Peel the cucumber and cut into slices. Place everything in a large bowl.
- For the dressing: mix the vinegar, the mustard, the honey, salt and pepper. Add 2 tbsp of oil little by little. Add the dressing to the salad and toss well. Place the salmon cubes on top and serve hot.

SMOKED SALMON TOAST WITH AVOCADO

For 1 serving:
1 slice of bread • olive oil • cream cheese • 1 or 2 slices of smoked salmon • ¼ avocado • ¼ lemon • pepper

- Toast the bread in the toaster or in the oven.
- Sprinkle the bread with a little olive oil. Spread the cream cheese on top.
- Place the smoked salmon on the bread.
- Wash the avocado and cut into half. Set aside the half with the core. Remove the peel and cut into slices. Place the avocado slices on top of the smoked salmon.
- Sprinkle the avocado with a little lemon juice.
- Season to taste with pepper and enjoy.

SMOKED SALMON TOAST WITH EGG

For 2 servings:
2 slices of sandwich bread • cream cheese • 2 to 4 slices of smoked salmon • 2 small eggs • 1 tspn chives • salt, pepper • ½ oz hard cheese

- Preheat the oven to 400 °F.
- Toast the bread in the toaster or in the oven.
- Spread the cream cheese on the bread. Place the smoked salmon on top so that it forms a circle. Crack an egg into the center of the salmon circle.
- Sprinkle with chive and season with salt and pepper. Add grated cheese to taste.
- Place in the oven and bake until the egg is to taste.

Chinese Fish Sticks

For 2 servings:

10 fish sticks • 1 leek • ½ can (6 oz) bamboo shoots • ½ can (6 oz) mung bean sprouts • 1 tbsp peanut oil • 4 ½ fl oz vegetable stock • 6 tbsp soy sauce • chili flakes • salt, pepper • 1 tspn starch

- Prepare the fish sticks according to the instructions on the packaging.
- Wash the leek and cut into thin slices. Drain the bamboo shoots and the mung bean sprouts.
- Heat the oil in a pan. Stir-fry the leek until soft. Add the bamboo shoots and the mung bean sprouts.
- Add the vegetable stock. Season with soy sauce, chili flakes, salt and pepper. Cook for 5 minutes.
- Mix the starch with a little water. Pour in and stir well.
- Serve the vegetables together with the fish sticks.

Adriatic Fish Stew

For 2 servings:

2 large tomatoes • 1 onion • 2 cloves of garlic • 1 tbsp olive oil • 4 ½ fl oz water • 1 bay leaf • marjoram • salt, pepper • 2 codfish fillets • ½ cup of vegetable stock • baguette

- Wash the tomatoes, cut into half, remove the stem and cut into half twice more. Peel the onion and the garlic and finely chop.
- Heat the oil in a pot. Stir-fry the onion and the garlic for 2 to 3 minutes.
- Add the tomatoes, the water and the bay leaf. Season well with salt and pepper. Put the lid on top and cook for 5 minutes.
- Place the fish in the pot. Add vegetable stock to taste. Put the lid on top and cook on medium heat for 15 minutes.
- After 15 minutes, season to taste with salt. Serve hot with baguette.

All rights reserved.

Publisher:
Iris Pilzer • Schärdinger Str. 50 • 94032 Passau • Germany • info@irispilzer.de

Photos:
Canva.com • Depositphotos.com

Disclaimer:
I'm neither a doctor nor a nutritionist. I tested all recipes and tips in this cookbook myself. But, as you know, people are different. This is why I can't guarantee that my recipes will work for you the way they worked for me. Food and diet is always trial and error. Think of this cookbook as a guide that helps you on your way to find the food you can eat without any problems.